Headstone in the Headlights

a second compendium of poems

BY Rick Taylor

Copyright © 2018 by Rick Taylor

All rights reserved. No part of this book may be reproduced in any form or by any electronic or mechanical means including photocopying, recording and information storage and retrieval systems—except in the case of brief quotations imbedded in critical articles or reviews—without the permission in writing from the author.

Cover & Book Design: Scribe Freelance
www.scribefreelance.com

Published by:
CEZNO PRESS

ISBN: 978-0-578-41688-5

Printed in the United States of America

Contents

Headstone in the Headlights 7
Narcissistic Ramblings 8
A Fall at Night 9
Time Capsule 10
Out to Lunch 11
A Freak Accident 18
Flights of Ideas 19
A Sailor Under Canvas 20
An Injected Memory 21
A Firm Connection 22
Hair And Bone 23
Daffodils 25
No Safe Haven 26
A Jewish Wedding 27
Chalice Bearer 28
A Parachute Over The White House 30
A Stain-Glassed Window 31
A Tribute to My Angels 32
A Triple Lament 33
A Warning Ignored 34
Any Poet Who Has Ever Been in Love 35
As Large as the Universe 36
Biff 37
Broken Rhapsody 39
Salvation at Last 40
Caul (Dedicated to Edna St. Vincent Millay) 41
Creature Comfort 42
Emboldened 43

Feeder	44
Finding the Groove	45
First In Line	46
Handsome	49
Go Slow	50
How Many Diversions?	51
I'm a Clone	52
A Book for All Ages	53
If This Were the 1800's	54
I'm Only Partly in Repose	55
Interface	56
Paige Turner	57
Perth Amboy Madonna	59
Poetry Is Fine	60
Sunset Years	61
Tarry Not	62
The Back Stairs	63
Bird of Ill Omen	64
A Fiery Space	65
A Pond in Winter	66
Whoosh	68
A Torrent of Words	69
Ramesses II	70
Raymond Carver	71
Rose-Colored Catastrophe	72
Musings of an Ancient Airman	73
Musings of a German General (1914)	74
No One Dreams Like I Do	75
A Metal Lunch Pail	76

Easter Release	78
Absence	79
A Poem to Lisa	80
Killjoy	81
Treading Lightly	82
Thumb Twiddling	83
Hedy	84
A New Neighbor	86
Precariously Close to Deity	88
Connections	89
His Excellency	90
The Furthest Point	91
Bicorne	93
Unsteady On My Feet	94
Eternal Eyes	96
A Golf Quitter	98
Walk or Run	99
Mrs Macomber	100
Blood Oath	101
Close Your Eyes	102
Ginger	103
Madagascar	104
Counterfeit Patriotism	105
Killer Dog	106
Just in Time	108
Two Rings	109
I Want to be a Gentleman	111
Irregardless	112
Lord Byron	113

Master of Kingdoms 114
Grind 115
Mysteries of Life 116
The Meatgrinder 117
After the Meatgrinder 118
Bugged Symbolism 119
A Biker in Blue Denim 120
A Marble Index 123
As Time Goes By 124
Aversion to Conversion 125
Blindsided 127
Classes for Retirees 128
Don't Miss the Bus 129
Floccinaucinihilipilification 131
Dreams by Moonlight 132
Early Disipline 133
Epiphany 134
Don't Kill the Republic 135
The Tree 137
A Glimpse of Humanity 138
At Heart a Shy Man 139
Self Love Loses 142
Hubris 143
Acknowledgements 144
About the Author 145

Headstone in the Headlights

At night, in a distant part of town,
though anxious for bed, I turn my car
into Mount Lebanon Cemetery instead.
Years ago, my classmate, buried there,
predicts that by spring he'll be dead.
Melanoma is the term he uses.
Our joyous college days are only recently past,
and a fateful diagnosis so close after graduation
comes much too fast.
At his funeral numbness effuses.

His headstone
shining in my headlights
confirms a passage of twenty years.
Good friend,
please excuse the delay.
During my time away,
Dana dies of ovarian cancer
after a brave fight
while I experience
the ravages of manic/depressive illness
before lithium puts things right.
Tears hidden in darkness
give reason for coming at night.

Narcissistic Ramblings

Lord Jesus, the expected renewal
hasn't come to pass.
I've been rolled on your lathe,
a painful honing
involving a razor-edged blade.
At the end, I expected to be a new specimen
ready for greatness as a writer
in any genre I dared to declare.
Lord, I hate to object,
but recent rejections by publishers and agents
and unanswered calls
seem to be my only bill of fare.
One acceptance at your behest
will permit me to jump the moat,
and scale the walls.

A Fall at Night

Asleep I hear your call.
HELP! PLEASE HELP ME!
I find you at the bottom of the stairs
after your fall.
Involuntarily, my words break free.
HOW CAN YOU DO THIS?
HOW CAN YOU DO THIS TO ME?
The list of woes is by then too long,
but you add three cracked vertebrae,
a second attack of shock lung and
renewed time on the ventilator
to the roster of what can go wrong.
Pull the plug, your sisters insist
until their voices are hoarse.
*Don't you see. Even if Dana survives,
the ovarian cancer must run its course.*
Still on the respirator, your eyes look up at me
as if to say.
*Do you really want to kill me?
Do you really want to blow me away?*

Time Capsule

Too often I elect to soar on
the wings of borrowed wit.
When I'm caught,
it's most distressing.
Some say there's no such thing as chance.
If so, I'm destined to remain unknown,
having missed the golden time of published works.
I'm old as the hills, hollowed out
from lowering empty buckets
into empty wells.
In sum, the hours of splendor in the grass
are fast compressing.
To avoid falling unknown
into the final pit,
I need the words of great poets and writers
to lift me up and free me from my faltering wit.

Out to Lunch

On TV news
I watch the Civil Rights marchers
and wonder
Where was I?
At Selma, Montgomery,
and other choices.
Songs instead of firearms
sung with resonate voices.
I can't get no satisfaction and
We shall overcome,
to substitute for rioting and burning,
all during my tenure in law school
when I was learning, learning, learning.

Two-hundred thousand in DC
hear King proclaim,
I have a dream
while I study civil rights,
always learning, learning, learning.
Then comes a brutal turning.
Bull Conner releases his dogs and hoses
on peaceful protestors,
and I ask myself—*where was I?*

Later, I see on T.V.
white and African-American soldiers
being blown to bits.
My plans in law school
will give the survivors fits.
I was in my last year

unconcerned about losing my life.
I'd substituted a thermometer for an M-16
as I planned the best time to impregnate my wife.

Out to Lunch—Part Two

I know what you're thinking,
but I won't use the word.
It starts with a *c*
and I can only wonder
whether it's applicable to me.
People with my propensities
should never don a uniform
in a serious way.
Yes, I avoided Viet Nam
and for that I feel rotten
as a lot of you know,
but no one was more likely
to return in a body bag
after confronting the foe.
My shortcomings
make me the worst Sad Sack.
No one is worse at reading a map
or following directions,
and no one is clumsier
even when the ground is flat.
The men in my platoon
would have taken bets
predicting how long
I could stand pat.
They'd picture me
stumbling into a pit of spikes
or stepping on an active mine
or getting lost on one of their "hikes"
or falling flat on even ground.
If by some miracle I did survive,
don't you see,
one of my officers
would have ended up fragging me.

Persistent Blues

My wife Mallory is in love with suffering.
She consistently captures the negative side.
She worries that I'll be killed in service.
You must wise up and quit the force.
Easy to say—
but I can follow no other course:
my father was a cop,
my son will be a cop, of course,
and with that kind of Irish lineage
there's no way I could quit.
Your children need you, she has said.
What good are you to them
if you end up dead?

A man of color my same age
gives goodbye kisses
to his young son and wife.
He has no gun or vest.
A black life to him is like all the rest.
He has no time for dissent or strife.
He falls asleep behind the wheel
weary from writing a memoir
about his life.

We get the call at 9:05.
A car overturned is leaking fuel.
We arrive in time
to find the driver alive.
Hanging with seatbelt in place,
he turns his head to look at me
revealing the terror on his tear-stained face.

We both know that at any moment
the car will blow.

I remember what my wife had said.
Your children need you in times like this.
So, too, I thought, *do his.*
Equal pain brings equal woe.

The rest of the drama is still a blur.
A knife from my boot
a seatbelt cut free
a black man saved from a fiery end,
who will soon enough
be a friend to me.

Puppet Master

A neighbor gives us
an unused puppet theatre,
huge in size with lights, a velvet curtain,
numerous puppets and a large stage.
It is just the right size to fit
into our oversized universe.
In no time, my sister and I
become the rage
by presenting full-fledged
puppetry on stage.
By the third neighborhood show,
certain of the participants
are too often involved in fights,
and I don't mean the audience,
my sister or me.
I'm talking about the puppets,
at least the few who begin acting
as if they want to be free
(free of strings, that is).
Each wants to be the main attraction:
Queen of the Nile, Hamlet,
King of Kings.
Gretchen in particular
begins pushing her rivals aside,
showing a bad motive and a bad temper
that are difficult to hide.
Phoebe, a gentle victim,
meekly defers to Gretchen's ego,
but Sanjo, Phoebe's lover, lets his anger grow.
On the night of our Christmas production,
our biggest show,
we find Gretchen rumpled and unmoving
at the bottom of her box.
I try to cross examine the chief suspect

but Sanjo isn't the kind of puppet who talks.
Nor can I accuse him of having done the deed.
He has no blood of his hands,
but, of course, murdered puppets don't bleed.

A Freak Accident

In a disastrous fall
while trimming a tree,
my big brother breaks his neck,
causing partial paralysis,
his wife's desertion,
and extended analysis.
The wharf by the river becomes the spot
where my brother, wheelchair-bound,
spends many a summer's day.
One morning that is particularly hot,
he sends me off to buy a Coke
from a dispenser some distance away.
I happen to turn in time
to see him roll himself off the quay.

The identification of his floating corpse
isn't a memory I can easily forget.
I'm convinced I should have foreseen
how determined he might get.
Yes, I was an unwilling pawn.
As a result, anger and guilt
and an absence of tears
provide the basis for a numbness
that has plagued me all these years.

Flights of Ideas

Flights of ideas, dark moods, manic upsurges, rapid speech.
In many cases (as with me) when lithium is applied
the patient's sane side is quickly restored.
By the time that happens, however,
many a career has been sabotaged
and many a friend has been gored.

A Sailor Under Canvas

Your eyes beautiful and deep
prompt in me a quiescence
much like that of a sailor under canvas,
prepped and ready for an endless sleep.
His plunge will come about but once,
which is nothing to despise,
whereas I must drown anew
each time I encounter those eyes.

An Injected Memory

Digital numbers
beside my bed
show seconds, minutes, hours,
a metronome of wakefulness
with each number burning red.
And then I hear it—
ghastly and forlorn
like the measured breathing
of something not of man born.
Guuush—guuush—guuush—guuush.
In a flash, I'm at the window
in time to see a hot air balloon
huge in size
and pink in color
pass before my eyes
on its way to the Regatta.
The birds that regularly herald
the morning's arrival with their cries
perch silent in the trees as though paralyzed.

A Firm Connection

How does a key determine
whether it's inside the right lock?
How does a sailing vessel recognize
that it's found the right dock?
Prescience--as with you and me.
We knew from the start
that we would exist like
two perfect peas
in one perfect pod.
What more could we stuff
into our perfect bubble?
If you say, "two cats,"
you're asking for trouble.

Hair And Bone

Dana selected cemetery plots
for both of us beneath a tree.
My three grown children now ask,
Why do you hesitate to go there?
They wonder whether there is some hidden motive
they cannot see.
In their minds, a minister
from nearby Sunnyside Church
should be the one to bury me.

My answer is always the same.
I explain that their mother's headstone
abuts an unused gravesite
set in place for me,
adding that it's somewhat unsettling
to visit because I'm reminded
of my own mortality.
I add that that my absence
can't really offend her,
since no part of her,
save casket, hair and bone,
is still in place beneath the earthen mound,
her soul having long since departed
for higher ground.

Still, they suspect
that my decision to remarry,
and move to a different town,
are the real reasons I've chosen
to leave their mother alone in the ground.

Naturally, I'm reluctant to tell them
that if they want to search
they'll discover my ashes have been pledged
with the greatest of care
to a columbarium in a different church.

Daffodils

Writing poetry? No small chore.
I stare at an empty page
for an hour or more
until my eyes are drawn
outside to the garden.
On this day
the daffodils stand at attention
in a perfect way.
Dana always kept daffodils near
because they provided notice
that she'd survived for another year.

A swelling in her neck
detected in winter presages her death
in the spring.
Despite this fatal sentence,
she remains active and brave.
Following her burial
on a sunny day in April
we place daffodils on her grave.

No Safe Haven

Keats once said that he would sooner fail
than miss the list of the greatest poets.
But his arrogance misses the point.
Even with his greatness confirmed,
his certain death could never be delayed.
Beggars and thieves with no great lines to ply
are treated in the exact same way.
Death can never be halted.
When it comes to the final day,
mere words are never exalted.

A Jewish Wedding

The parents of the bride,
having been raised like me
on the Christian side of the room,
give evidence of their wonderment
as they study the traditions
associated with a Jewish groom.
Out on the patio of a local Club,
each guest observes an unusual sight:
a diamond-shaped box
for the release of butterflies.
It will be a moment of drama
for the transmogrified larvae
soon enough anxious to take flight.
I'm later told that the butterfly release
isn't part of the Reformed tradition.
The ceremony ends
when the groom with a lurch
stomps on a cloth-covered glass.
As he ascends the aisle,
arm and arm with his new bride.
both appear to be as happy
as any couple married in a church.

Chalice Bearer

MINISTER:
I need a chalice bearer for Sunday's service. The slot has gone empty and it's got to be filled.

CANDIDATE:
I'm not the man for the job. I was in the war. I can't even estimate the number of men I killed.

MINISTER:
Still, I have this need.

CANDIDATE:
But I can't fill it. I can't forget what I've done. To this day I see each face. One victim couldn't have been more than fourteen or fifteen. Many a night I see his blue eyes full-open and staring.

MINISTER:
Don't you see? Your guilt is a measure of your caring. That was years ago, in the war. Back then you were fighting to keep your country free. This is now. You are a good man. I want you up there at the altar with me.

CANDIDATE:
I recognize your need. But this I cannot do. I'm a sinner of the worst kind.

MINISTER:
A sinner of the worst kind is one who doesn't repent as you have done. As far as I'm concerned, you're heaven sent. I'll give you a few days. Talk it over with Emma. I'm hopeful she'll convince you in time for Lent.

EMMA:
And so, he came to me, his wife, expressing all his fears. I knew what he was going through even after all these years. One night in bed I touched him during one of his dreams. He grabbed me by the throat, while splitting the silence with one of his screams.

CANDIDATE:
Emma, I could've killed you. I often sneaked up on enemy soldiers at night. I'd strangle them with my hands. In my nightmare, I was seeing you as one of those and it gave me quite a fright. It was a nightmare of the worse kind. Be careful in the future. Good wives are hard to find.

EMMA:
As a chalice bearer, he was great. He wasn't the first war hero to have been led through the gate.

A Parachute Over The White House

A parachute
over the White House
slowly descending.
Men below in blue suits
scurry about,
not knowing why or who,
but pretending that they do.
I hold onto the straps
to let them know
I'm unarmed,
but I can see that one man
is scoping me.
My chest holds the red dot
at the end of his beam.
Then it hits me.
With a loud scream
I alert God that there's still time
to turn my dramatic descent
into an exciting dream.

A Stain-Glassed Window

Always she is there,
her countenance highlighted
by gleaming fluorescence
with Joseph behind
and the shepherds close by.
She is ever-adoring
through war, holocaust,
hurricane and flood,
a symbol of peace
not just for our pompous congregation
but for all humanity
although many here insist
on exclusivity.

A Tribute to My Angels

Driving alone at night
during a winter storm,
I fall asleep at the wheel.
Three taps on my shoulder
that I feel
awaken me in time
to avoid driving off the road.
In my mind's eye,
I see my car explode
as I burn to a crisp inside.
Was someone or something
with me on that ride?
Did the invisible person
have a magic wand
and a pair of wings?
To say the least,
I'm not used to dealing
with supernatural things.
Then, later, I learn about
a different candidate
known as the Holy Spirit.
Because He's clearly
the best guardian I've found
I'm going to do everything in my power
to keep Him around.

A Triple Lament

James, Natalie and Sal
arrive on the set
of *Rebel Without a Cause*
feeling light-headed and free
unaware that you as their director
intend to violate all three.
You exude the necessary charm
to seduce young Natalie
with plenty left over for James and Sal.
How could they have idolized you?
Anticipated fame
from *Rebel* should never
have justified such a course.
And what is worse,
your nefarious acts
assured all three a tragic fate
after exposing each to your evil seed—
near Paso Robles James is killed
when his sports car crashes at high speed—
at Santa Catalina at night
Natalie drowns beside her yacht
—and Sal is murdered on Sunset Boulevard
on a day that is oppressively hot.
Like Old Nick you asserted a fee
put in place to destroy all three.

A Warning Ignored

In the chancel
during the exchange of vows
the bride sees her milk-white gloves,
elbow-length
soaked in blood.
Later in the limo the gloves
are perfectly clean.
Is this an omen?
If so, what does it mean?

Any Poet Who Has Ever Been in Love

Any poet who has ever been in love
writes about it in verse or sonnet
so long as the feeling is appropriately fresh,
and there's a willingness to reflect upon it.
As for me, when it comes to the disaster known as *love*,
I've always been inspired to describe its terrible scourges.
If I'm able to write effectively about what I've felt,
perhaps then I'll fend off any similar urges.

As Large as the Universe

In this aged body
enthusiasm smolders unseen
ready to be ignited by simple verse
that reflects on subjects
tiny as a robin's egg
or as large as the universe.

Biff

When the name Elizabeth,
becomes too difficult
for her sister's childish tongue,
Biff is the name Jan chooses
to apply even when the two
are no longer young.
Jan is the first
to hear of Biff's Oscar bid,
and the first to console her
when she loses.
Subsequent mental problems
end a promising career.
Jan receives the final blow
when Biff's body is found
beneath her apartment-house window
on the cold, hard ground
seven flights below.

Her funeral is not well attended.
After all, Hollywood moguls and their starlets
have little time for sentiment.
Many years before,
a young starlet jumped from the Hollywood sign
after choosing the letter *H* as her final perch.
Her body was found by accident.
There had been no concerted search.
No one seemed to miss her,
and no one acknowledged her despair.
As with so many victims who followed her,
no one really seemed to care.

Those who don't reach the upper ranks
reserved for the very best
are easily discarded
as Jan can well attest.

Broken Rhapsody

In the early years
I'm living a dream—
a wonderful spouse
a fantastic house
with a golf club nearby.
It's a perfect life
or so it seems.
Too soon we learn
that we're living a lie,
but like Rasputin
I refuse to die—
stabbed, shot, poisoned and drowned,
I keep bobbing back up
ever hopeful that my battered body
will someday be found.

Salvation at Last

Leave it to a pixie from Texas
to turn my life around.
She is aware of the tough turns I've taken,
and loves me nonetheless.
A sage would say she is *God-given*.
Who am I to second guess?

Caul (Dedicated to Edna St. Vincent Millay)

Your caul at birth foretells
what your later life confirms,
but your literary greatness also produces
drunkenness, cirrhosis
and a drug addiction
you work so hard to fight,
all preceding a fatal fall
down a staircase late at night.
We know of Anne Sexton's agonies
and Ernest's explosive stand.
We've read of Sylvia's release
with her children close at hand.
Still, even with such consequences,
I'd accept a writer's lot,
and I'd do it without a caul,
which shows how much gall I've got.

Creature Comfort

In 1967, a film
is taken in Northern California
at a desolate place
by two adventurers.
The one named Patterson,
spots a female creature,
ape-like and walking upright
with a human-like face.
Estimated height: eight feet.
Estimated weight: eight-hundred pounds.
She has a massive body
and a wheeze-like yell
combined with a gigantic stride
and an unpleasant smell
that all the perfumes of the Orient
could never dispel.
Darwin is debunked.
This product of natural evolution
is walking in the woods,
not yet officially discovered.
Obviously, these hairy creatures
have evolved from apes
whereas man is unique,
God's special creation,
a miracle of miracles,
a wonder of wonders,
and feature by feature
unmatched by any other creature.

Emboldened

Through the front window
I spot a hawk perched
on a far-off branch
on a winter night,
a dark silhouette
against the moon,
silent and unmoving
at a significant height,
the bold protagonist
of Act One
of my little play.

Act Two begins with
a rabbit in the snow
a wee, furry thing
bounding across the white surface
down below.
I shouldn't tarry long, he is thinking.
There's always danger nearby
and I'm too young to die.
It's just that the evening breeze
is so invigorating.
There's so much to look forward to.
I'm ready to face the universe.
I'm emboldened.
I feel—
There is no Act Three.

Feeder

Above our back deck
is a bird feeder
with seeds that show
through the glass.
Woe to us
if we let those seeds run low.
Our feathery customers
soon become bitter
perched on railing, sill and branch
with tilted heads and stifled twitter.
It matters not that this feathered picket-line
can devour a full container of seeds
in less than an hour.
In their minds, the bill of fare should be constant
even though the cost of seeds might be high.
We can almost hear their full-throated constraints.
You feed that damned dog twice a day.
Why do you favor that hairy beast?
We'll give you all the devotion you crave
if our food supply is adequately increased.
A dog cannot streak across the sky.
Nor can it feather a nest.
A dog cannot chirp or twill
and, certainly, it will never molt.
And so, we suggest you keep that container full
or be prepared to suffer
a full-scale avian revolt."

Finding the Groove

White and pink
this flower
extends its pedals upward
nimble
flexuous
as if to touch a lover's lips.
Even in the deepest swamps
and darkest bogs
the orchid's upward lift persists.

First In Line

How big is Heaven?

Now there's a question that will test the knowledge.
of a professor in a small Christian college.
Sometimes I think my students are overly aggressive.
I hesitate to answer, stalling for time,
convinced that the onslaught will be excessive.

The reason I ask, Professor Glib,
is that Heaven had better be prodigious,
considering the number of people
who have passed on since Eden was closed
and I'm not particularly religious.

I answer cautiously.
I expect that Heaven is infinite,
with room for an infinite number of souls.

They are temporarily calmed by my answer.
But not for long.

Professor Glib, who gets into this Club?

I answer quickly.
Well, first off, Heaven isn't a Club.
There's no high wall.
Anyone who accepts Jesus will be rewarded,
and Heaven is the highest reward of all.

I can see that my students aren't satisfied.

For many that will sound good, Professor Glib,
but what about the people who haven't been exposed to the good news,
such as the Muslims or the Jews?

Admittedly, I'm groping, but I answer as best I can.:
Many survivors who have returned after once being dead
describe a soothing light a short distance ahead.
Before they reach it, they choose to reverse course
and return to the land of the living instead.

I keep going.
My theory, which, mind you, isn't part of the Nicene Creed,
sets forth that when those same souls later move into that light,
they'll see Jesus standing there in all his glory,
at which point they'll undoubtedly accept Him,
no questions asked, end of story.

My students are stunned by this reference to a near-death experience,
but soon enough discover that there are other theories that they must
also test.

Professor Glib, where will this journey take place?

I know I'm groping but I try to do my best.
Many survivors describe the experience as being similar
to a passage through a tunnel or tube.

My answer doesn't slow them. I'm impatient to have this end,
but I don't want to be rude.

Will all of us have the same opportunity to observe that light?

Now I'm creating answers out of whole cloth:

*Yes, every non-believer will have the same opportunity to see Jesus and
make things right.
On the other hand, I suspect that many ISIS fighters will be so aghast
at the prospect of missing their seventy-plus virgins
that they'll ignore Jesus and move right on past."*

My students laugh briefly; then another speaks out.

*Is salvation available for the reprobate
who has filled his life with sin and evil tricks?*

I must be creative even though the question isn't new.
*Although Jesus was crucified to forgive our transgressions,
repentance is also part of the mix,
as is purgatory, at least in my view.*

The questions keep coming.
*Professor Glib, regarding purgatory, how long will it take for a person to
get through?*

Not exactly, a safe opening,
but I will do what I can do.
*I suspect that it depends on the magnitude of the sins.
Women who have ended their pregnancies intentionally
will probably have a chance to meet the children they've chosen to avoid.
The rest of us must face any souls we've killed or destroyed.
Time-wise, figure on at least two months, give or take.*

It's pure poppycock, of course,
but how can any single professor know what kind of responses to make?
Professor Glib, what do you know about Hell—

—excuse me for interrupting, I say,
but I think I just heard the bell."

Handsome

I was born without a hand.
For the longest time I was fine without it.
My friends would compensate
by throwing the ball to my good side.
Then, you insisted on a prosthetic device
which added a claw I was unable to hide.
Those same friends began to ridicule me at camp.
Have you ever tried to catch a grounder
with a clamp?

Go Slow

Azalea,
Daffodils,
Forsythia,
Rhododendron—
go slow, go slow
let the breeze tell of these.
Let sunlight's dappled glow
dance over my outstretched arm.
The day is mild, not the least bit hot.
In response to a bounding squirrel,
Ginger yanks on her leash
thereby ending my reverie
on the spot.

How Many Diversions?

From the moment of our birth
the Holy Spirit begins tugging at us
like the moon pulls at the sea.
If we give in to this holy motion
the resulting caress
will set us free.

I'm a Clone

At the age of twenty,
I've been robbed
of a significant number of years
since I must subtract from my lifespan
the years attributable to my donor,
a man of sixty, or so it appears.
It's very disheartening to be told
that at the age of twenty I have the life span
of an eighty-year-old.
Under the rules, I'm unable to marry.
Even if I were, who'd elect to marry a geek
whose life might cease at the end of the week?
We clones live in large dormitories outside Vegas.
I'm told that there will be no sex,
and that spiritually I have no soul.
Still, I suspect that salvation
will be available
when judgment day finally looms.
If not, I can only ask
why did they put Bibles in our rooms?

A Book for All Ages

When the head of our book club
insists that we review my poetry book,
I, of course, am thrilled,
but also, somewhat wary.
What if my poetry isn't held
in high esteem?
The thought of a negative assessment
is deflating as well as scary.
Before the event, I tell them of my fears.
I hint that if the hook is applied
I'll probably get sick or burst into tears
(was I really kidding?)
During the review
most of the comments
are presented in positive stages.
I begin to feel puffed up
with the thought that some of my poetry
might somehow survive through the ages.
Then, the senior member of our group
admits that he keeps my book in his john
and was running out of pages.

If This Were the 1800's

If this were the 1800's
and I were a British gentleman,
I'd laugh at my rotten love-life
and venture off to the Sudan.
To counter Lady Willard's inclination
to ignore me in favor of a richer man,
I'd button on a blood-red tunic
and lead a charge at Omdurman.
If any woman
finds me to be a bore,
I'd trudge off to South Africa
and kill a hundred Boer or more.
But no such relief
is available
in this modern world we face.
I'm too weak to flog a Shiite,
and too old to love with grace.

I'm Only Partly in Repose

I'm only partly in repose.
Remaining is a restlessness
engendered by an unfulfilled desire
to write great poetry and prose.
The inspiration comes each time I see
a hawk in flight
or watch a sunset's dwindling flame.
If God intended to stifle
my creative fire
why would he arm me
with this strong conviction,
and overpowering desire?

Interface

Hydrangea provide a memory of Chautauqua
that returns with a snowball's bite
offering a fragrance similar
to my mother's perfume
which I discover
every time she leans over my bed
to kiss me good night.

Paige Turner

On stage *the Airmen of Note*
in blue uniform offer an array
of instruments, mostly brass,
that produce an ear-piercing din
that to me is quite crass.
Right off, I'm reminded to my chagrin,
that Jazz, particularly loud Jazz,
isn't something I prefer
but it's too late to head for the exit
without being charged with a sin.

And then Paige appears,
a beautiful singer in a slinky gown
bare at the shoulders and full length
matching in color her auburn hair
which is hanging loose,
and in one fell swoop
I'm hooked on the music,
Jazz or not.

There's no thought of leaving.
I'm glued to the spot.
And, Oh, can that woman sing!
All her numbers produce
an eruption of applause.
and the audience becomes restive
each time she withdraws.
Eventually, she appears in blue uniform.
with her hair, her beautiful hair,
formerly luxurious and hot,

scrunched up into a tiny knot.

No matter;
even when she changes course,
in my mind's eye
she'll still be in that slinky dress
which makes me think of many things
(none related to the U.S. Air Force).

Perth Amboy Madonna

Your image appears quite suddenly
on a second-story window.
In awe the gawkers come—family members,
neighbors, holy sisters, priests—
several times a day
all with hands outstretched
to touch your image before turning away.
Are you too much with the world, gentle virgin?
Should you have insisted that the pilgrims not come near?
These same hands that came to worship you
have turned your image into a smear.

Poetry Is Fine

Poetry is fine,
but I must recognize
that unlike Keats
there are no nightingales
in my verse
singing with *full-throated ease.*
But, O, if the fates give me
a work of poetry or prose
blessed with a publisher's positive kiss,
I'll lose all inhibitions
and willingly drown
in a sea of contentment and bliss.

Sunset Years

Laughing children.
Endless summers.
Welcoming grass.
Sitting on my bench
in the park,
I speculate that
most of the children
playing in front of me
can count on receiving
sixty plus years
whereas I'm
sixty plus already
with little room
for forward projections.
Despite my limited reach
I have no objections.

Tarry Not

When the service ends,
I say a few words to the Pastor,
then scurry down the front steps
anxious to be on my way,
ignoring spring's blossoms as I go—
rhododendron, azalea, daffodil and tulip.
I'm anxious
to speed home to my poetry
so that I can write about
rhododendron, azalea, daffodils and tulip
beside a silent phone
in a tiny room,
sometimes inspired, but always alone.

The Back Stairs

The back stairs
dark and confining
project downward one flight
to the spot where my Grandfather waits
to cook my breakfast
in a kitchen that is sterile and bright.
Until he dies, he's always there.
*Two eggs on toast
sunny-side up.*
Mother tolerates him
but only barely.
He thinks she's treating him unfairly,
by insisting that he climb
three flights on bad legs
to use his own facilities.
This regimen prompts
objections by phone
to relatives on my father's side
that I happen to overhear
when he thinks he's alone.
When I describe the complaints
to Mother, she enlightens Father
who has some cutting things to say.
*How could you betray him?
He cooks your eggs every day.*
Ashamed at what I'd done,
Words don't come.
I simply look away.
But I never again
think of betraying Grandfather
after that fateful day.

Bird of Ill Omen

At one time, I think
the evil bird's coverage
is reserved for victims
anxious to take chances—
a kook who spelunkers, a speed demon,
a mad-cap looking for the razor's edge.
Now I know differently.
The wretched bird,
ugly and cruel,
didn't hesitate to rub out
my youngest daughter
struck by a drunk driver
on her way home from school.

A Fiery Space

O mighty whale,
don't let them belittle you
with worldly measurements.
Your essence isn't meant
for this world,
but is instead connected
to a corner of another world
where madness and immorality converge,
a place where
the blackness of your soul
can blend with
the blackness of the universe.

A Pond in Winter

Ginger and I are cozy
inside my car
parked away from the pond,
but not too far.
It is the spot she chooses
for watery plunges in the summer.
Despite the cold,
the surface is unfrozen.
Leafless trees lean forward
with purpose
to observe their grotesque reflections
in the turf-colored surface.
The cloudbank above winks its eye
to reveal the sun's bright cornea
behind the plain grey color
of a winter sky.
In the back seat,
Ginger is anxious to take
a watery romp
despite the change in season.
How do I explain to a dog
that grass, once lush and green,
is yellow and brown this day for a reason?
For Ginger such explanations
fall on deaf ears,
red, floppy ears.
For her, the pond is inviting
irrespective of the season.
For her, the best romp
is one that comes real soon.

Pond water is every bit as inviting
in January as it is in June.

Whoosh

In the Great War
bloated rats devoured corpses
unreachable from the trenches.
Only recently
warehouse workers near Verdun
open a hidden door
to hear a WHOOSHING sound
produced by a million rats or more,
queuing up
for the next inevitable war.

A Torrent of Words

My Muse, once aroused,
releases a torrent of words
overpowering and unceasing
until my brain threatens to burst.
The solar system
becomes marbles in a dish.
Waves on water
become scales on a fish.
Well-intentioned Muse,
please release me
from this curse
before the floodgates burst open
and I'm drowned in my own verse.

Ramesses II

Egypt's Abu Simbel
expertly carved into nature's wall
offers four colossal figures
proud and tall
each depicting Ramesses II
in a deified state,
strategically placed
at the temple's front gate.
When the rising waters
of the Aswan dam
challenge this temple eternal,
a movement springs up
to save the famous site
by lifting the giant figures
to a specified height.
To ignore Abu Simbel, they say,
is to disregard the Pharaoh's
continuing renown.
In the end, the temple's saviors conclude
that the superhuman colossi
should be given a lift
instead of being left there to drown.

Raymond Carver

Like me, Raymond,
you have a disastrous early period.
Your *line of demarcation,* you say,
comes when you decide to put the bottle away.
Until then, you admit that you're full of rage.
You want the reader to know
that during your *gravy days*
you turn over a new page
when your writing begins to flow.
I've had my own ugly times
that produced a history I can't hide.
Unlike you, my renewal occurs
when the proper medication is applied.
Pundits say that overriding pain
helps writers reach the highest rung.
That isn't much solace to you
since you died so young.
Hopefully, I'll produce writing
that will qualify as being great.
If not, please remember
I got started late.

Rose-Colored Catastrophe

During my parents' outdoor party
I hide in my secret place
behind the wall
that abuts our oversized patio.
The hidden space
is a perfect place to hide,
but as an extra precaution,
I duck behind the rose bushes
that grow on the side.
Bloody Mary's
and chitchat are offered
to at least twenty-five
of my parents' closest friends.
From my hiding spot
I hear my father whispering,
and try not to giggle or laugh.
I hear him say,
Darling, I love you a lot.
In place of the familiar refrain,
pink-tipped fingernails,
not my mother's,
brush his open hand.
I remain silent and restrained
as the two saunter off
to opposite ends of the patio
where both assume casual poses.
It's the start of a tragic summer.
It is also the genesis
of my hatred of roses.

Musings of an Ancient Airman

An incessant sputter from the sky
brings forth the memory
of my first solo flight at night.
Fortunately, there is time for reflection.
Burley on my left, Cornfield on my right,
mustachioed and leather jacketed,
wingmen assigned for my protection,
but at the end of the day
it is they, not I, who are lost.
Proud Yank in the RAF,
I'm convinced I can never die.
Still, I become shattered
each time one of my comrades
is shot out of the sky.
Annie, my wife,
who knows what such musings are worth,
waits patiently beside me
for a sign that I've come back to earth.

Musings of a German General (1914)

Our massive hordes
smash through with ease.
After the surrender,
French resistance forces take over.
Sabotage and murderous acts prevail.
In retaliation,
we put many of the culprits in jail.
At the same time, we begin executing hostages,
first, three or four,
then, many more.
Despite these tactics
the guerilla attacks continue as before.
How is it that the execution
of so many prominent citizens
can be so easily ignored?

No One Dreams Like I Do

No one dreams like I do.
My nightmares are so extensive
that shutting them down
becomes an impossible chore.
In the case of murder, robbery, rape or incest
my demons always give their best
and then offer more.
For murder, they insist on holding the gun.
If rape is the theme,
while the victim whimpers and begs,
my demons step forward
to hold down her legs.
The detestable demons I conjure up
are an ugly lot.
In truth, however, I must put up with them.
They're the only demons I've got.

A Metal Lunch Pail

A metal lunch pail,
encountered by chance,
like the one Father carried
during his B&O years,
purchased at O'Hurley's,
and O, the memories it brings:
Train rides with Father at the throttle
telling stories that are never drab
of Casey Jones and other such heroes
as my sister and I sit listening in the cab.
Every engineer, he says,
is forced into the role of killer.
The crazies know
we can't stop on a dime.
In any encounter with a train,
they're going to lose every time.

One evening he arrived home bowed over,
staring at his shoes.
There was another suicide, he said, stifling a sob.
Mother had a quick reply.
Dear, you've experienced such tragedies before.
Horrible as they are, they come with the job.
His grey eyes kept staring straight ahead.
This one was different, he said. *The woman*
was holding a baby in her arms.
Both ended up dead.
Mother speculated that the *poor woman*
probably didn't want to leave her child behind
to be jockeyed back and forth by the Fates.

Father speculated from a different direction.
Her love was probably unrequited, he said.
She killed the child to punish her lover whom she hates.
In her mind, the child was better off dead.
Which is it? Nobility or disgrace.
At the end, one viewpoint prevails.
When the train struck the woman and her child,
she was completely off the rails.

Easter Release

Birth in Bethlehem,
Baptism.
Crucifixion
followed by
an ascent into glory.
If a time span of two thousand-years
hasn't weakened the basic story,
perhaps it's time
to recognize that the account
includes a wonderful plot.
Perhaps it's also time
to stifle smorgasbord pursuits
that permit selection
by a *believer* of any creed that suits.
A triune God
remains a God of love,
and Mary is clearly a virgin
when Gabriel comes calling.
Indeed, the tomb is empty
when the heavenly angel appears.
Such precepts are not appalling.
On the other hand,
if we continue to revise
the sacred teachings
and the lessons they embrace
Jesus will soon become a hollow icon
incapable of granting grace.

Absence

Today he lives behind a hollow stare.
His pupils are gray and opaque
like the cows' eyes
we "borrowed"
from dissecting class.
His lips move,
but no sensible
dialogue can be heard.
No longer capable of fending off attacks
this once brilliant lawyer
is dead in his tracks.

A Poem to Lisa

What will we do?
A first-Sunday without Lisa.
Without paninis.
Without wine.
Oh, misery, you are now defined.
The poetry was important, but
the crucial part
was the magic
that came
when we dined.
I'd like to end this poem
with a final tribute
to her wonderful eatery
but nothing rhymes with Scheherazade
(isn't that odd?).

Killjoy

Ketchup-red tie,
crisp, white shirt
a gold disc in each cuff
a pin-striped suit
with perfect creases—
then, my wife appears
and with one finger
highlights a grease spot
causing an SSSSTTTTT sound
as my confidence releases.

Treading Lightly

I've always wanted to write a poem,
so stirring, so passionate
as to melt the stars,
but the sick hurry of my life
causes me to eddy back and forth
in a way that impedes my best intentions.
At first, my thought is that
in the right setting with the right bent
I can achieve my dream
with very little effort spent.
Such delusions are favored
by procrastinators and hypocrites.
In the end, I must admit
that my poetry will never cause much of a fuss.
That is a hard nut to swallow
for those of us who are seventy plus.

Thumb Twiddling

Even now I see them,
Dana's twiddling thumbs,
first one on top, then the other.
I watch this exercise as I drive.
The doctor will tell us that the lump in my neck
means the cancer's in my bloodstream.
He'll say he can no longer keep me alive.
Transfixed by her twiddling,
I come close to blocking out her voice.
You're numbing out again, she says.
You'd better be prepared for what comes.
You have no choice.
From the start, Dana has been full of dire predictions.
I've gotten used to each horror story as it comes.
But how can one small lump in her neck turn the tide?
Is it true that we've reached the final hurrah?
Is this what has caused the twiddling thumbs?
In his office, the doctor tells us why and how.
When his dire prognosis comes,
I look down to discover
that I'm twiddling my thumbs.

Hedy

Cursed with exceptional beauty
and a long life,
you arrive in Hollywood
ill-prepared for the upheaval and strife
that awaits you there.
The moguls assign unending workdays
while forcing you to take
uppers and downers
to keep you at night asleep
and in daytime awake,
thereby deadening your brain.
How tragic!
In the early years, your brain
inspires a patented invention
used on ships of the U.S. fleet.
But the moguls scoff
at such acts of brilliance.
Brainpower disrupts
the only objectives they seek.
Old age, they know, will affect your beauty,
starting with your face.
Their objective is to assign
as many movie roles as possible
while your fan-base and your beauty
are still in place.
Bombshell is a documentary
that presents a view
of what happens
when a lovely victim like you
is subjected to continual abuse

before being thrown onto the refuse pile.
We study with horror a face
no longer able to smile
ravaged as it is by multiple facelifts.
Your beauty, once said to be timeless,
has in the end no time for you.

A New Neighbor

Pithecanthropus, better known as *the Java man*
showed up in our neighborhood
with his wife and children in tow.
He was wearing a suit,
probably as a device to hide the excessive hair
that covered his body from head to toe.
It seemed obvious from the start
that he probably wouldn't fit in,
although his wife, a Catholic girl,
was quite charming.
Chances were good that my neighbors would find
his slanted forehead, jagged teeth
and body odor
to be somewhat disarming.
He also had a bad habit
we all struggled to ignore
of spitting in church,
not in a handkerchief as you might expect,
but right there on the sanctuary floor.
Fortunately for him,
his wife, a wealthy woman,
provided a large annual pledge.
Well, right away
he expressed with some insistence
a desire to join Sunny Meadows,
a golf club well known for being stuffy.
As head of the Membership Committee,
I suspected that his request would get off track.
At first, I tried to dissuade him
by pointing out that his arms

were much too long to swing a club,
but he wouldn't get off my back.
To my amazement, he sailed right through,
And here's what makes it far from funny.
If this distasteful man can join
without a flub
because of his wife's money,
I'm convinced that I should join
a different club.

Precariously Close to Deity

Over the years, we've become very capable.
Remember that scientists designed and built
an atomic bomb almost from scratch.
The next step was to locate
a place to drop it,
and now that the beast is out of its lair,
they've begun to think of ways to stop it.
You say *look to the Middle East.*
In my view, it will take two superpowers
doubling-down
to bring about an effective peace
and that means teaming with Russia.
Will wonders never cease?
The kneejerk reaction is to say,
No way can that be.
Russia has always been our enemy.
I'm no Commie, but I'm here to say
I'd rather be slightly pink
than blown away.

Connections

The cat is out of the bag,
and this feline won't stop mewing
about mania's fireworks,
depression's black hole,
and a drug known as lithium
that is prescribed in time
to save my troubled soul.
Soon I learn that my condition
may be a badge of honor.
In *Touched with Fire*
Kay Redfield Jamison
writes that bipolar disease
has affected most great poets
who begin by generating a mania
that is impossible to hide.
In her book on Robert Lowell,
a bipolar poet, she points out that
brilliance and mania
most often exist side by side.
When lithium is prescribed
to smooth out my troubled moods
and end my living hell,
I'm concerned that my creativity,
such as it is, may disappear as well.
There is but one answer: *Time will tell.*

His Excellency

In the National Gallery
he stands in vertical canvas—
blue uniform, gold epaulettes,
white facings, red cuffs
medals on his chest,
a hand that reaches
inside his vest
(presumably for effect
and not to hold up
his stark-white breeches).

The Furthest Point

In Mark Twain's view,
Sir Walter Scott's novels
were the primary cause of the Civil War.
Twain's special thing
consisted of Knights jousting in "days of yore."
Twain wasn't fully serious, of course.
Still, his ideas carry a sting.
In the Civil War, chivalry was an ideal
both sides sought to perfect.
We remember the sculpted frieze
in the National Gallery
showing Colonel Robert Gould Shaw
astride his horse, ramrod straight
leading his African-American troops
to their tragic fate.
Other images come to mind.
Sheridan's ride.
Custer's last stand.
When the bugles sound
and the artillery commences
chivalry demands that each man
throw himself forward
out of the trenches.
If many deaths occur
that is perfectly okay
since casualties are a byproduct
of the bugle's call
that each hero must obey.
Our women now ask,
Why do they do it?

How many dead men must we anoint?
Who among the men
has the nerve to tell them
that war is a contest between men
to see who can piss to the furthest point.

Bicorne

I expect we all know what a Unicorn is.
But what is a Bicorne?
Few would guess that it's a two-cornered hat.
Imagine that.
Fewer still would associate such a hat with Waterloo
or remember that it was the type of hat Wellington doffed
when the battle was won.
Some would say his hat was dumb.
I doubt that the Iron Duke would agree.
His troops well understood his gesture.
To them it signaled victory.
Wellington, favored black,
avoiding gaudiness in all respects
as he remained astride his horse.
In battle, Napoleon favored
a uniform of lower rank
along with his Tricorne,
a three-cornered hat, of course.
Their French and British subordinates
are dressed to the nines with egos to match—
capes of animal fur, feathers on top of hats, high boots,
Bicornes, Tricornes, medals by the batch,
swords at the ready.
Who could doubt their bravery?
Who could say they weren't steady?
And who would fail to notice their despair,
until the smell of gunpowder once again
filled the air.

Unsteady On My Feet

It's either neuropathy
or weak ankles
or just plain old age,
but I'm unsteady on my feet.
If there's a banister nearby,
I always use it.
If there's a sense
that my balance is off,
I don't abuse it.
Yesterday at the National Gallery of Art
I went from one banister to the next
as I counted step after step after step
after step after step after step, to the top
And I didn't fall. Not at all.
My experience on my stepson's stairway
wasn't as good.
He had fashioned a series of steps
downward to the Potomac from his house
extending several feet,
steep steps, many steps
ending at a stone-covered beach.
His visitors, mostly my family,
were safely down
and sitting in the river with beers in hand.
I'm the last one still above,
and I'm not about to admit
that the descent is beyond my reach.
Unfortunately, a rope
is substituted for a banister
and the rope is absent

close to the bottom.
The expression is *ass over teacups*
and now I know why.
I end up flat on my back
looking up at the sky.
As soon as the crowd determines
that I wasn't hurt
they let out a unified laugh
even while I'm still lying flat in the dirt.
My stepson, John, soon
arrives with a canoe.
There is nothing funnier
than the sight of an unbalanced geezer
trying to step into one of those—apparently.

Eternal Eyes

Cranston and I draw fire
coming from a tree line above us.
We fall on our stomachs,
while responding in kind.
Unable to see your position,
we're firing blind.
During a lull in the action,
I begin belly-crawling upward
determined and slow
while Cranston provides cover
from the roadway down below.
I crawl until our faces almost touch.
You've fallen face-forward in the dirt.
Startled by the wound in your head
your blue eyes are full open
(apparently, you never expected to be dead).
Both eyes are locked and frozen,
with a hole in between round and clean.
I'm so sorry. So very sorry.
You are far too young to die
(at most, fourteen or fifteen).
Thankfully, we'll never know
whether it was my bullet or Cranston's
that provided your third eye.

But you knew then
and you know now,
or so it seems.
Your blue eyes continue
to contaminate my thoughts

and shine at me in my dreams.
Don't you see?
If Cranston had done the killing,
you'd have no continuing interest in me.

A Golf Quitter

One day I said, *That's it!*
I've teed up my very last ball.
Others have eye-hand coordination.
let them have it all.
My customary foursome
was eager to know
the basis for this drastic action.
I concocted two stories,
neither of which was true,
not by a fraction.
First, I said that during
one particularly bad round
I looked up to see vultures
circling round and round
over my golf game,
several feet off the ground.
The second told of chats
with representatives of Titleist
who offered me two thousand a year,
plus an unlimited supply of golf balls
not to wear one of their hats.
My foursome laughed, of course,
but I never went back.

Walk or Run

Jog, run or sit.
Be cowardly or brave.
Any approach we choose
will ultimately lead
to the same open grave.

Mrs Macomber

After Francis's fatal accident on Safari,
Margot came back to the States,
and made it known to the guys at the Club
that she was ready to go out on dates.
I was sucked in by her beauty.
She took it upon herself
to re-shape what she called
"my boring bachelor life"
by proposing somewhat boldly
that she expected to be my wife.
However, at the slightest provocation,
she would resort to scathing words
intended to make me feel stupid and small.
Her unpredictable trigger-finger
and disarming guile
encouraged me to swear off women,
especially her, at least for a while.
My willpower proved to be extremely weak,
which, of course, is nothing new.
My boycott lasted less than a week
until a brunette, gorgeous and long legged,
sat down in the very same pew.

Blood Oath

You are a glance,
conveyed through eyes
that open your soul
to me.

You are a voice
funneled through tinged lips
showing beautiful teeth
as you speak.

You are a dream
with a scent that is real
and flesh that is felt
through the deepest sleep.

When I awaken
you come to me
for all ages and all times,
immortal.

Close Your Eyes

Close your eyes.
Do you see the faces?
Drifting down slowly
one after the other,
on a black background
behind the lids–
a bearded warrior
with eyes gouged out,
head of wolf
with snarling snout.
When my fear
is most pronounced.
the bloody faces,
angry, raging, pouting,
find me
one by one.
What's that you say?
You see them, too?
Considering that I'm bipolar
and manic
I wonder—
what the hell is wrong with you?

Ginger

Because I'm not a poodle
you think I'm hard as nails.
Well, red-coated labs have feelings, too,
especially those of us
who've got some class
(as I certainly do).
How would you like it
if I were to stand behind you
at all times with a plastic bag?
Oh, I know it's just for droppings,
but my blood turns to ice
when a crinkling sound
proves the appearance
of that barbarous device.
Give me the old days
when a steamer
could just stay where it lay
as a territorial guide-on
to keep all canine encroachers at bay.

Madagascar

Last night
I travel to Madagascar.
I'm an experienced dream traveler,
but I've never traveled to Madagascar before
so I wonder--*What emotion*
secured my passage to that distant shore?
We are camped by the Mangoky,
a river that runs swiftly and deep,
and in sight of the Ankaratra Mountains,
when a band of renegades
interrupts our sleep.
I'm the last to die, so I wonder—
What recent events are ruining my sleep?
Was it your refusal
to make love to me
last night
or was it the ice cream and tuna fish
I consumed
before turning off the light?

Counterfeit Patriotism

In a bar in DC
we encounter a boastful bore
who gives us the "benefit"
of his thoughts on the war.
He reviews the *unconscionability*
of the Tonkin Gulf attacks.
McNamara and Johnson
are *dead on,* he says,
when they push for an increase
in total troop strength
based on those dreadful Tonkin facts.
In addition, reliance on body count
is for him a strategy without a flaw.

Did you ever serve? I ask.
Without flinching
he stands up to his full height and says,
*I think you'll agree that my position
has no flaw.
I've lost two cousins,
and stand ready to sacrifice my brother-in-law.*

Killer Dog

It's hard when a first impression
turns out to be flat wrong.
It's doubly painful when the wrong impression
relates to your very own dog.
Ginger is an eight-year old red lab.
She stops strangers which we happen to meet
who want to highlight her beauty
right there on the street.
Dear, kind, feminine Ginger.
Convinced that a sweet disposition
accompanies her beautiful features,
I'm always pleased to hear such praise.
At home she's always full of kisses
a practice that has continued
from her earliest days.

And then it happens.
A dove is caught in our screened-in porch.
Although the avenue of escape lies wide open,
the terrified bird elects instead to fly to and froe.
I step onto the porch with the objective of
showing the bird the correct way to go.

Ginger has other plans.
With a guttural growl I've never heard before
she lunges forward when she sees that the bird
has made the mistake of landing
close by on the floor.
Even though a chair blocks my view,
I see feathers flying upward.

Next, I notice the dove breathing its last
while lying on its side several feet from the door.
I'm devastated, not just because
the bird is dead,
but, also, because Ginger,
once known for her beauty and grace,
had elected to become a criminal instead.

Just in Time

Lithium, the gold standard of bipolar treatment,
puts my life back on its hinges.
As I endeavor to restring the beads,
I wonder, with no little fear,
whether the urge to create,
hopefully inspired by an underlying genius,
will, because of the medication,
dissipate and disappear.
Good news prevails.
Not only does the renewal
preserve my creative bursts of fire,
it also extinguishes the red-hot coals
tied to wanton and unwholesome desire.
What an advantage to sufferers like me
that lithium finally is here.
Think of Sylvia Plath, Virginia Woolf, Hemingway
and so many others who died without knowing
that their mania was nothing to fear.

Two Rings

Mussolini and his mistress
are seen hanging like slabs of meat.
In my case there must be no remains,
he says, and imposes a schedule
that will be difficult to meet—
a double-ring ceremony,
followed by a double suicide,
followed by a double burning.
I'm a lowly Lieutenant
but he trusts me to do the burning,
now that the tide of the war is turning.

The smell of sweat, excrement and urine.
in the bunker becomes more intense every day.
Until he collars me, I'm all set to run away,
but now I must stay
to supervise the cremation
on the appointed day.

The first step is to retrieve
two wedding rings
at Gestapo headquarters
stolen from two murdered Jews,
husband and wife.
When I hand the rings to him,
his hands are shaking
and his eyes are full of tears.
He turns toward his living-space
and quickly disappears.

Later, I learn of genocide against the Jews,
so shocking as to be impossible to hide
and I think of the two murdered victims.
It's ironic that symbols of their love,
a love that will forever abide,
played a key role in the sequence of events
leading up to the fateful burning
and the double suicide.

I Want to be a Gentleman

I want to be a gentleman,
the change, I know, will bring me bliss,
the kind of gentleman
who writes great poetry
and steps out of the shower to piss.

Irregardless

Irregardless
is in the dictionary;
a discovery that makes me sigh,
because it makes me wonder
about other teachings
that might turn out to be a lie.
If this keeps up, George Elliot
will be a woman
and George Sand won't be a guy.

Lord Byron

Brilliant as well as lecherous.
Handsome as well as treacherous,
you were deemed a degenerate
even before you took Augusta,
your half-sister, into your arms.
Augusta was no exception.
Most women who encountered you
were seduced easily by your manly charms.
Empty coaches at your funeral
were part of a blacklisting most vile.
Beyond caring, you are now in another world
where you walk in beauty
immune from insult and rage,
knowing that the same critics,
who defiled you during your lifetime
have made you after death
the idol of your age.

Master of Kingdoms

Master of kingdoms
created with a poet's eye
I'm no less a demi-god
than Gilgamesh, Alexander
or Tamerlane so long as I'm able
to lift my pen and write from the soul
using words that will carry me
and my vast hordes,
toward any earth-changing goal—
across ancient seas,
over stony defilements,
only stopping to sharpen our swords
or to greet poor Shakespeare
who in my presence
is at a loss for words.

Grind

You tell me to stop grinding—
as if your command alone
will make my teeth ungrate.
You tell me to eat only one
pork tenderloin,
while leaving the other on my plate.
A conversation like this
invariably vexes
since it highlights
the glaring disparity
between the sexes.
If a man wants change,
he must chip away
persistently over the years
on the hard rock
of his personality
until a new face appears.
If a woman wants change,
she simply orders the nearest man to do it.
The thought of changing herself
is so foreign
she's not anxious to pursue it.

Mysteries of Life

The mysteries of life
are explained in an ordinary garden.
One seed,
a push toward the light,
the emergence of a petal most fair,
plus raking, weeding, sowing, deadheading—
it's all there.

The Meatgrinder

Psychotherapy once a week
for eight long years
with you as my shrink.
An opportunity for you to learn
that my life was a heap
of smoldering ruin.
With mania consuming me,
my brain raged in a way
that made it impossible to think.
However, I've come to see
that your delay in diagnosis
may have been a blessing after all
now that I've learned about the link
between madness and creativity.
That being the case,
a prolonged period in the meatgrinder
might have been an appropriate call.

After the Meatgrinder

The Bible uses a perfect choice of words to describe
the effect of what I call the meatgrinder.
In much wisdom is much grief;
and he that increaseth knowledge,
increaseth sorrow. Eccles. 1:14.
I've had my share of sorrow,
and the wisdom that has come
has brought with it a new spirituality.
The Bible tells us that His voice directs us
and I've come to think I hear it loud and clear.
Since I'm hearing voices,
my wife has begun to suspect
that I may have slipped another gear.

Bugged Symbolism

During a pruning exercise,
I remove a bird nest from our tree
causing tiny mites by the thousands,
to abandon their comfort zone
and scatter in a struggle to be free.
I think of Native Americans,
whose habitat gave comfort
—clear waters, rolling grass,
purple mountains,
and buffalo herds so huge
it took a day for them to pass.
Like the mites, the Native Americans
assumed they would remain unmolested
anywhere they chose to stay,
and then, they watched in horror
as the world they loved
began gradually to slip away.
Once exposed, the mites are easy prey.
My plan of extermination is so thorough
very few get away.

A Biker in Blue Denim

Archibald! Conrad shouts.

Why does he always pick on me?
I'm a defrocked priest,
a biker in blue denim,
a joke for all the world to see.
By bellowing my name
that strutting peacock,
causes all attention in the barroom
to be focused on me.

Conrad continues.

Why did all miracles end after the Apostles died?

Why ask me? I shout.

*Because you're the only one
who knows what it's all about.*

All right, I say, but if I accept this challenge
and do not fail,
you'll owe me the best prize
I can think of—
a full pitcher of German ale.

Done! Conrad shouts.

Then I start my pitch.
Constantine observed

*two separate heavenly visions
and went on to witness
his enemy suffer various mishaps
culminating when a bridge across the Tiber
just happened to collapse.*

There is silence for a moment.
Then someone shouts,
Conrad, I think you've met your match.

Not yet, not yet, Conrad coos.
If that's all you've got, Archibald, you lose.

Now I'm mad because he's attempting
to buck the hitch, as they say out west.

All right then, *Think of the Godly gale
that gave the Armada its final test.
The Lord favored England on that day
until a tiny group of colonies
with God's help challenged the empire
in a far different way.
And where are the Nazis today?
They were the real test—
one of the ugliest evils
ever spawned on earth.
They were obliterated entirely
at God's behest
thereby giving the world a rebirth.
And look at the historical figures
who have passed the test—
Washington, Adams, Jefferson, Lincoln,
Grant, Wellington, Churchill,
FDR, Eisenhower—all are famous*

*for miraculous accomplishments,
yet, not one was blessed with a saintly birth.*

Conrad's face went from flushed red to pale
and right then I knew I'd won my ale.

A Marble Index

In Florence I stand before
a marble index, smooth, cold, huge in size,
a young man-god, naked to the world.
I study his eyes.
They show a far-off stare, dead serious.
He also provides an eye-opening physique,
an anatomy of bulging muscle and bone
so faultless as to be mysterious.
Such perfection in ancient times.
Doesn't that seem odd?
You answer quickly.
Don't you see?
The hard chisel that Michelangelo held
was guided by the hand of God.

As Time Goes By

I'm at a piano bar
alone and out of town
writing poetry on a paper napkin.
The inveterate brunette
in a red evening gown
is singing at the keys—
you must remember this—
reminding me
with full-throated ease
that time goes by.

Aversion to Conversion

At sixty-four I've got a lot of life left in me.
They told me to get out, to leave Germany,
but I didn't listen.
My Iron Cross First Class
will protect me, I said.
Now I see that the vestiges of my past valor
had gone to my head.
Here I stand naked and full of fear
in a long line of terrified men
who, like me, must know that death is near.
Is mankind truly capable of such evil?
At first, I thought that God would protect me.
My conviction came
after studying Psalms
like this one—*He will not suffer*
thy foot to be moved.
The Lord shall preserve thee
from all evil. (121st)
and this one—*Yea though I walk*
through the valley of the shadow of death
I will fear no evil: for thou art with me;
thy rod and thy staff they comfort me. (23rd)
Poppycock. Pure poppycock. Don't you see?
My foot has been moved
and I've been herded into the valley of the shadow.
Yet, no one comes to save me.
Most of the naked men in my line
use their hands to cover their private parts.
I want to say, *Fools, following death in the "showers"*
your manhood will be burned away well before

they pile your remains onto a waiting cart.
Modesty does not make sense here.
Considering that the Babylonians, Syrians,
Assyrians, Romans, Nazis, and the Palestinians
have all been out for blood,
if you want to save your Chosen People, Father,
you'd better bring on another flood.

Blindsided

The choir gathers in the Narthex,
then proceeds down the center aisle
with the ministers close behind
while the organ pounds and then—
a prayer of confession,
a sermon from the pulpit,
and, finally, the closing hymn.
Numbed by the pomp
and circumstance
and overwhelmed
by the sights and sounds,
it's not surprising, not at all,
that no one remembers
the married minister's dalliances
with the pretty choir member
on the couch in the upstairs hall.

Classes for Retirees

Classes for retirees
prompt my walk to the university
over five blocks,
past St. Paul's Cathedral
and the Catholic school beside it
that disgorges girls on this day
much younger than my daughters
in plaid skirts and knee socks,
giggling and shrieking on their way
impervious to fall's colorful display.
I think of the walk from Melwood Street
to law school many years before,
innocent, with a young bride,
unaware of the jealousies
and backstabbing
that large law firms would provide.
Like a spotted fawn before the pack,
or a toddler stumbling toward the edge,
I move blindly ahead.
When I'm near drowned,
spit out, dumped on the rocks,
the medication known as lithium comes
just in time to relieve any further shocks.

Don't Miss the Bus

Do we Christians have a lock on things to come
because paradise supposedly is available only to us?
If so, a lot of capable people
will miss the celestial bus.
For those of you who insist
a candidate can only reach the Father
through the Son,
I present this scenario,
just for fun.

Imagine a lengthy corridor or tube
leading to Heaven.
In near-death experiences, many have said
that just before turning around,
they noticed a soothing light up ahead.
I posit that Jesus stands in that light.
If so, who could refuse to accept Him
at first sight?
A decision to accept a living god
is certainly no disgrace,
especially when the candidate will be seeing Jesus
in all his glory face to face.

What of the Jews? The answer is simple.
One Messiah is like any other.
When they recognize Jesus
standing before them,
they certainly will have made the grade.
What about the Muslims?
They may be reluctant to adjust,
thinking that reaching Mohammed
and a bevy of waiting virgins further on

is not an option, but a must.
In the parable of the laborers does Jesus imply
that non-believers who wait to accept him
on the way into heaven are still entitled to seats on the bus?
Or will they be obliged to face a waiting period,
known as purgatory where they will face a final honing
not required of the rest of us?
No one knows for sure
what will happen during the journey into glory.
When it comes to describing matters
that will occur on the way
every candidate can be his own jury.

Floccinaucinihilipilification

Floccinaucinihilipilification
is a word you rarely spy.
I wonder why.

Dreams by Moonlight

Years ago, after kissing Leola
at lakeside under a radiant moon,
I was encouraged to think
that our love wouldn't end any time soon.
Marriage, children, a circular drive
were pleasant images that I could foresee.
Naïve and young as I was, however,
I was unaware of the moon's inconstancy.
Eventually, Leola couldn't hide her preference
for significant family money,
the type of wealth that only a mogul could provide.
When a suitable candidate appeared,
I was quickly brushed aside.

To win her back, I persevered in my pursuit,
and in time became quite wealthy.
Still, even after numerous poignant demands,
I couldn't talk Leola into leaving this guy,
which means I've had to change the strategy I'd planned,
and wait for the bastard to die.

Early Discipline

In East Pakistan
a skeleton is unearthed
that appears to be extremely old.
Being an expert on bones,
especially the ancient kind.
I'm immediately told
to perform studies
to determine
the age of the find.

The bones turn out to be
430,000 years old
according to my test.
They belonged to a young male
who died of a wound in his chest.
In my opinion,
the bones belonged to an unruly teenager
who acted up in the family cave.
I suspect that he became one of the first
to ignore the standard admonition
that fathers in those days routinely gave.
Don't make me come back there.

Epiphany

Epiphany in Greek means *shining forth*.
James Joyce's beautiful seabird,
a young woman standing midstream,
was an epiphany he'd seen and heard.
Some say it occurs when something mundane
is transformed into something extraordinary.
Others say it is a sudden glimpse of humanity
often discovered in poetry.
The relentless surf in *Dover Beach,*
becomes a metronome governing our lives.
For me, when the connection is discovered,
the pleasant shock feels like my hair
is beginning to rise.
For a moment, the outside world blurs.
As a poet, little else really matters
until the next epiphany occurs.

Don't Kill the Republic

65 million years ago
a meteor drops from the skies.
Most reptiles are destroyed
and from then on
mammals are on the rise.
It is evidence of a plan
formulated by a God-centered universe.
Deny it if you can.

In 1776 we take on the British,
the largest military power on earth.
No wonder we're skittish about the British.
It'll take a miracle
to show what we are worth.
Yorktown will do.
It's part of a divine plan.
Deny it if you can.

Jackson at New Orleans.
Lines that are stretched thin
defeat a much larger force.
How "lucky" we are to win.
Is our Republic favored?
Is this part of a plan?
History gives the answer.
Deny it if you can.

Sheridan at Cedar Creek.
Lincoln will lose in '64
if this defeat isn't turned around.
Sheridan alone arrives to turn the tide
after his famous ride.

It is part of a plan.
Deny it if you can.

The Tree

The maple tree in the churchyard
puts great stress on its roots.
It stretches upward sturdy and tall
while displaying
numerous weighty branches
and a massive trunk,
the heaviest part of all.
And yet, this tree will never fall
even after a hundred years
so long as mankind's caprices
and nature's blow
stand aside to let it grow.

A Glimpse of Humanity

Some writers say
that short stories
in their own special way
provide a glimpse of humanity.
Hemingway consistently
shows us the way
with characters like—
Margot Macomber,
a rich bitch with a sure aim;
Harry, who fights death
while driving his wife near insane;
Ole Anderson, the Swede,
unwilling to run from his killers
even though he is able;
Joe, who learns new truths
about his dead old man
a short distance from the stable;
Nick Adams, a damaged vet,
fishing alone on the shore
while trying to forget
the horror of war.
Each wonderful character shows us
what an author's insight and understanding will bring
and each is anxious to jump into our psyche
and pull every available string.

At Heart a Shy Man

Joe Adams was not the type of man
any woman would adore.
At heart he was a shy man,
meek might be a better word.
Because he lived alone
and was quite poor,
no one was the least bit surprised
when he was drafted to serve
in the Vietnam war.
Still, Joe didn't complain a lot.
In Boot Camp, he learned
after consistent perfect scores
that he was a crack shot.

While on leave,
Joe wanted to impress
the girls at home
with the Marksman's medals
he'd earned on the range.
Despite the decorations
their low opinion of him
didn't change.
To the girls at the Bistro,
he remained a geek to ignore.
They didn't correct that view
even when he told them
about his placement
on an elite Army shooting team
that soon would be going on tour.

At the first shooting exhibition,
a beautiful Israeli agent,

approached him at the end of the day
to ask him to spy for Mossad
whose objective was to assassinate
former Nazis who couldn't be brought to justice
in any other way.
She was very persistent
and pointed out
that with a high-powered scope,
he'd be able to score
from a very safe distance.
She also said he could remain on tour,
since his travels provided perfect cover.
After she volunteered
to be his lover,
he offered no further resistance.

The plan worked well for the first three hits.
He was beginning to feel he was part of a team.
Soon he was assigned a fourth victim,
a former Nazi mass murderer,
whose family was otherwise clean.
After no little effort,
Joe found his assigned target
with his granddaughter
playing in the yard on the ground.
Joe waited for the child
to leave the scene
then dispatched his target
with a single round.

It didn't take Joe long
to report to his lover
who immediately ascertained
that something was very wrong.
His words expressed
his deep chagrin:

Do you realize the fix I'm in?
You never told me
he had an identical twin.

Self-Love Loses

Some time ago,
I was told
that to love others properly
self-love must come first.
I envied those with peace of mind,
who could love with impunity,
without feeling the curse
of mood changes like mine.
Because of my negative thoughts
self-love had been hard to find.
When told that my bipolar condition
for certain
was the cause of my woes,
I tried lithium
and found that 2 pills a day
were enough to raise the curtain.

Hubris

*My Friend… you wanted to talk about hubris.
In the extreme it exudes a power we cannot trace
like dark matter in the universe
that holds a billion galaxies in place.
Think of Napoléon
who went from corporal to Emperor
after an inspired and feverish run.
Meanwhile, men and women close to him
whose hearts were quickly won
began spinning in orbits
around his all-powerful sun.
Think of what we could accomplish if,
in a resigned and deliberate way,
we relieved ourselves of all self-doubt
and let our self-confidence have full sway.*

*You won't like my response, my Friend,
because, in my view, such a strategy
would invariably result in an unhappy end—
assassination in the case of Julius Caesar
or burning beyond recognition
in the case of Hitler
or (in the case of you know who)
poisoning on a distant isle.
It's best, I think, to set hubris aside
in favor of meekness
and an unassuming smile.*

Acknowledgements

As was the case with the first volume of poetry entitled *Never Alone in a Cemetery* Kendra Adkins of Four Seasons Book Store in Shepherdstown has provided crucial advice and encouragement. Shannon, my good wife, has provided countless hours and loving assurances in fulfilling her role as editor.

About the Author

Rick Taylor is a graduate of Pitt Law School and Denison University who presently resides in Shepherdstown, West Virginia (near the battlefield of Antietam). His poetry has been featured in Eureka and in the California Quarterly. "A Time to Walk the Ocean Floor" and "As Large as the Universe" appeared in Volume 25, Number 2 (2006) of Westview, a publication of Southwestern Oklahoma State University. In November of 2005 "Foxfire" was awarded third place in the 2005 Pennwriters Poetry Contest. On January 2, 2010, his poem entitled "Never Alone in a Cemetery" appeared in the Pittsburgh Post-Gazette. Several of his poems were recently published in Good News, a local newspaper. He previously published a book of poetry under the title *Never Alone in a Cemetery* containing just over one hundred poems, which was first on the best seller list in Shepherdstown upon its release. Copies of his books can be obtained through Amazon. Switching genres, he recently completed a manuscript of some thirty short stories entitled *Against The Grain*, which is approximately 80,000 words in length.

www.ingramcontent.com/pod-product-compliance
Lightning Source LLC
Chambersburg PA
CBHW071403290426
44108CB00014B/1672